Breakthrough Living
Deleting Limitations and Multiplying Success

Table of Contents

Believe you can and you're halfway there.

— Theodore Roosevelt

Chapter 1. Introduction

Welcome to a world of unleashing potential like never before with our Special Report: "Breakthrough Living: Deleting Limitations and Multiplying Success." We invite you on a joyful journey of personal development where you're not just dreaming big, you're achieving bigger. This isn't an academic treatise; it's a tangible toolbox and encouraging guidebook positioned to help you break through your limitations and multiply your successes. This report is about you, your goals, and the unimaginable future that we can help you craft! It's time to erase your self-doubt, add zeroes to your performance metrics, and truly live a life defined by breakthroughs. Don't just exist — it's time to thrive! Buckle up and prepare for an exhilarating ride into a reality where everything you aspire for is within your reach. Enthralling, enlightening, and absolutely life-altering, this Special Report is not just a purchase—it's an investment in infinite possibilities.

Chapter 2. Unveiling Your Inner Power: The Start of the Journey

Our journey begins with an exploration of the intrinsic dynamism that exists deep within your being, which we will refer to as your 'Inner Power.' This power is an amalgamation of signature strengths, unique talents, profound passions, and intuitive wisdom that you possess. The key to living a breakthrough life lies in identifying, understanding and optimizing this powerhouse of potential. The more deeply you probe into the depths of your inner self, the clearer this source of energy becomes, guiding you towards a life marked by success and fulfillment. Let's unfold the multi-faceted narrative of inner power, and begin the journey towards breakthrough living.

2.1. Embracing the Concept of Inner Power

Inner power can be conceived as an enduring reservoir of energy, a force that fuels your dreams and drives your actions. It is a unique combination of your mental, emotional, spiritual, and physical capacities. Each of us carries an untapped potential inside, and revealing this unexplored dynamism forms the very basis of our journey. Despite its innate presence in every individual, it remains latent until a conscious decision is made to awaken it. This chapter delineates the importance of inner power, its various components, and the process to tap into it effectively.

2.2. The Components of Inner Power: Recognize, Reflect, and Realign

Inner power is broadly composed of four elements: Mental power, Emotional power, Spiritual power, and Physical power. Each of these offers unique strengths and when harmoniously integrated, they give rise to a formidable energy unconstrained by limitations or barriers.

1. **Mental Power:** It is the substructure of rational thinking, intellectual capacity, creativity, and learning ability. It allows you to comprehend, interpret, and create solutions to challenges that come your way.

2. **Emotional Power:** It comprises emotional intelligence, empathy, resilience, and emotional resilience. It enables you to handle circumstances with an empathetic approach, remain resilient in the face of adversity, and bounce back from setbacks with renewed vigor.

3. **Spiritual Power:** It includes spiritual beliefs, moral values, ethical principles, and a sense of purpose. It serves as your inner compass, guiding you in making righteous choices, drawing moral boundaries, and finding a higher purpose in life.

4. **Physical Power:** It pertains to physical vitality, endurance, and overall health. It supports you in maintaining optimum health, fostering a healthy lifestyle that further adds to your mental and emotional wellbeing.

2.3. Awakening Your Inner Power: A Structured Approach

Awakening your inner power involves a structured three-step approach — Recognize, Reflect, and Realign.

Recognize: The first imperative step is to acknowledge and appreciate your unique qualities, strengths, abilities, and talents. This is achieved by introspection, self-analysis, and feedback from people who know you at an intimate level.

Reflect: Once these distinctive traits have been discerned, you should reflect upon how they affect your daily actions, reactions, and decisions. Meditation, contemplation, and journaling are effective tools for gaining insights into this process.

Realign: The final step is to realign any mismatch between your unique strengths and present life conditions. This requires altering your routines, habits, and attitudes that are hindering the optimal use of your inner power.

2.4. Harnessing Your Inner Power: A Transformative Exercise

Harnessing the strength of your inner power calls for a regular practice of introspection, self-renewal, and self-improvement. This involves an in-depth understanding of your core strengths, values, and interests, and consciously utilizing them in your daily life. It also calls for eliminating self-doubts, fears, negative self-talk and any psychological barriers that undermine your inner power.

In conclusion, unveiling your inner power is the maiden voyage into the riveting journey of breakthrough living. It is about recognizing and embracing your true potential, that unique force that drives you toward your dreams and transforms them into reality. It is this force that not only enhances your performance but also adds a layer of authenticity to your actions, making you distinctive. Your inner power is the beacon that enlightens your path, illuminates your purpose, and transfigures every hindrance into a pathway to success. By unveiling your inner power, you start incorporating sustainable changes that gradually build up into a life of breakthroughs. The journey may seem daunting, but remember: every milestone you reach is a testament to your courage and determination, and every step leads you closer to your ultimate success. Your journey has just begun! Brace yourself for the adventure, for it promises to be immensely rewarding in terms of growth, transformation, and self-discovery.

Chapter 3. Understanding Limitations: Self-Imposed Barriers and How to Dismantle Them

The attempt to comprehend our own personal barriers begins with the crucial understanding that the mind and its attitudes, whether positive or negative, play significant roles in the shaping of our reality. It demands an inquiring exploration into the territories of our thoughts and beliefs, unraveling the very threads of self-influence, which say much about our limitations.

3.1. Sub Chapter Heading: Understanding Self-Imposed Limitations

Self-imposed limitations can be thought of as the barriers we construct within ourselves, often unknowingly, that prevent us from being the best versions of ourselves. These obstacles typically reside in the realm of the mind, woven together by the tailoring threads of our fears, self-doubt, past mistakes, and negative societal stigmas. They are, by nature, restrictions of self, invisible yet firm boundaries that confine us in a sphere of self-perceived inability and underachievement.

Think of these limitations as self-imposed prison walls, high and oppressive, silently muting the potential that simmeringly resides within us. They are subtle yet impactful, hampering our growth, mutilating our self-esteem, and muting our aspirations. Breaking down these walls calls for thoughtful introspection, nuanced understanding, and active dismantling of these barriers.

It's crucial to highlight that the most insidious aspect of these limitations is their self-perceived nature. We've constructed these mental barricades ourselves, often unknowingly, molded by our associations, experiences, and habits.

3.2. Sub Chapter Heading: Identifying the Constructs of Self-Imposed Limitations

The roots of self-imposed limitations are often in the recesses of our subconscious, interlaced with our thought process, nourishing negative self-talk, and perpetuating fears and doubts that stand as colossal hurdles in our path to self-realization and achievement.

These barriers take multiple forms:

- Fear of Failure: This is a pervasive factor that induces inaction and encourages a defensive approach towards goal realization. We often avoid taking risks out of fear, which confines our growth potential.

- Negative Self-Talk: This refers to the internal dialogue that underlines our thoughts with negativity, disarming our confidence with harsh criticism and downplay.

- Social Conditioning: Often, societal expectations or stigmas shape our thoughts. Our orientations are influenced, and we naturally limit ourselves to what we 'should' be doing, rather than what we 'could' be doing.

- Past Experience: Negative experiences or failures from the past can trigger a defensive mechanism, resulting in us erecting barriers to future efforts and exploration.

Recognizing these constructs is the foremost step towards disarming these limitations. Your awareness of these barriers shines the light of understanding upon them – illuminating them and revealing them for what they truly are: obstacles that are by no means invincible.

3.3. Sub Chapter Heading: Strategies to Dismantle Self-Imposed Barriers

The elimination of these self-imposed limitations is not a casual endeavor. It demands methodical introspection, honest self-resources assessment, and active cognitive reconditioning. Below are some strategies to help you weed out these self-sanctioned barriers:

- Self-Awareness: Increasing self-awareness through introspection and mindfulness helps identify these self-imposed limitations. Meditative practices can facilitate this awareness.

- Change in Thought Process: Recondition your thought process. Cultivate an abundance mindset instead of scarcity mindset. Replace fear of failure with learning and growth perspective.

- Reframing Self-Talk: Pay attention to your inner voice. If it errs frequently to negativity, reframe it with constructive criticism, positive affirmations, and entrepreneurial zest.

- Constructive Social Environment: Surround yourself with people who inspire positivity, growth, and trigger ambition. Their influence could significantly change your perspective, leading to breaking down of self-imposed limitations.

- Leveraging Past Failures: While past experiences can feed into fear, they can also fuel growth if we adopt the right outlook towards them. Learn from past mistakes rather than letting them hold you back.

As we hope to realize, the liberation from self-imposed limitations purely hinges on conscious, active efforts and a sustained reformation of our internal dialogues and perceptions. By allowing ourselves to use these barriers as stepping stones rather than stumbling blocks, we can ascend to a realm where limitations become illusions and potential, a boundless ocean.

In the succeeding sections of this report, we shall embark on more in-depth explorations of these strategies to unwrap the layers of self-imposed restrictions and reveal the potential reservoir within. Remember, the only real prison bars are those we allow to remain around us. Embrace the challenge, break free, and join us in living a breakthrough life.

Chapter 4. Retraining The Mind: Building a Success-Oriented Mindset

In the bustling arena of life, our minds remain both our most powerful ally and potentially our most formidable foe. It is a complex, intricate system that shapes our thoughts, beliefs, emotions, and actions. Concurrently, it is responsible for our perception, interpretation, and responses to various life circumstances. This cognitive map not only steers the course of our daily interactions and experiences but also sets the stage for our overall life trajectories. By retraining our minds, we can develop a success-oriented mindset: a potent tool in transforming our lives and jettisoning us far beyond the domain of limitations and into a cosmos of infinite possibilities.

4.1. The Significance of a Success-Oriented Mindset

Laying the groundwork first, we need to recognize the significance of a success-oriented mindset and its pivotal role in reshaping our lives. For instance, consider an iceberg, where only a minor section is visible above the water surface. The vast majority of it remains submerged—unseen but incredibly potent. Our conscious mind can be compared to the visible part of the iceberg, and our subconscious mind to the expansive, submerged portion.

While our conscious minds seem to regulate our daily activities, it is, in fact, our subconscious mind that holds formidable sway over our emotions, attitudes, and behaviours. For instance, the repeated narratives we tell ourselves—our beliefs about what we can and can't do—reside deep within our subconscious. Consequently, developing a success-oriented mindset requires diligent analysis and alteration of these deep-seated beliefs—similar to navigating the profound depths of the iceberg.

4.2. Understanding the Power of Neuroplasticity

A concept pivotal to comprehending the process of mind retraining is neuroplasticity—the brain's incredible capacity to modify its own structure and function in response to experience or injury. In other words, our brains aren't fixed entities but dynamic structures that can change, adapt, and learn throughout our lifetime. We could think of the brain as a malleable entity - like clay; it can be kneaded, shaped, and modelled as per our wishes. Profound, isn't it?

Neuroplasticity empowers us to redesign our minds, thus actively influencing our thoughts, emotions, and behaviours. For instance, when we persistently dwell on negative thoughts, we reinforce negative neural pathways, leading to a pessimistic mindset. But the inverse is also true. By fostering positive thoughts, we can encourage the formation of positive neural connections, thus facilitating a success-oriented mindset.

4.3. Techniques for Training the Mind for Success

In this fascinating journey of retraining our minds, we'll explore several strategies that can help us pave the pathway to success and create an exciting tapestry rich in positivity, productivity, and potential.

The first technique at our disposal is Visualization. Visualization is a potent tool used by many successful individuals across various fields. It is an exercise that involves picturing our life goals vividly, thereby fostering motivation to convert these visions into reality.

Visualization reflects the proverb, "Seeing is believing." This technique not only solidifies our goals in our minds but also serves as a constant reminder of our aspirations, nudging us to work diligently towards them.

Next comes the power of Positive Affirmations. By continuously reinforcing positive beliefs and statements about ourselves, we can rewire our subconscious minds and alter self-imposed limitations that hinder our pathway to success. Regular repetition of these affirmations has a potent impact on our subconscious mind, slowly transforming the negative belief systems housed within. Though it may seem rudimentary, the potential for change that this method can unlock is truly colossal.

Cognitive Reframing forms another cornerstone in our journey towards developing a success-oriented mindset. This technique helps us shift our perspective and reinterpret negative or adverse events in a positive or neutral light. By consciously choosing to view our circumstances from a different lens, we can recalibrate our responses and emotions associated with these situations. Over time, this pattern of reframing experiences positively can train our minds to cultivate an inherently positive outlook, thereby enhancing our resilience and our chances at success.

Lastly, the practice of Mindfulness denotes living in the present moment without judgment. This approach aids in reducing stress, increasing focus, and strengthening emotional regulation—all vital contributors to a healthy, success-oriented mindset. By remaining aware and accepting of our present state without being swept away by thoughts of the past or the future, we enhance our mental capacity to deal with current challenges effectively.

4.4. The Journey Towards a Success-Oriented Mindset: An Ongoing Process

The expedition towards a success-oriented mindset is not a temporary escapade. Instead, it is a lifelong commitment and an ongoing process. Retraining our minds and ingraining new patterns of thought requires time, perseverance, and consistent effort.

It may entail swimming upstream against the current of established negative thought patterns. However, the reward lies not just at the end of the journey but also in the journey itself. As we progress, the world around us starts to transform. We begin to embody an aura of positivity, charge headfirst into challenges, and welcome failures as stepping stones towards success—unleashing our true potential and transcending limitations along the way.

Through this transformative journey of mental reprogramming, we equip ourselves with the most powerful tool—a well-crafted, success-oriented mindset. Armed with such prowess, pressing forward towards a life of breakthrough living becomes not just a theoretical possibility but an attainable reality. Hence, there lies no exaggeration in saying that retraining our minds for success forms the very bedrock upon which the edifice of breakthrough living is fortified.

Chapter 5. Strategy Formation: Blueprint to Breakthrough Living

In our quest for success, realization of our potential, and multiple breakthroughs, one of the pivotal elements we need to meticulously look at is the formulation of a clear, robust, and effective strategy. A strategy is akin to a map that navigates the complex terrains of aspirations and ambitions, assesses the available resources and skills, and smoothen your path towards the coveted breakthrough living. It's not just the route illuminator but also a compass that ensures you always head towards the right direction. In this chapter, we will dive deep into the art and science of effective strategy formation to unlock the doors to extraordinary success.

5.1. What is a Strategy and Why is it Important?

A strategy is a detailed and comprehensive plan designed to achieve a long-term target or an overall aim. It differs from tactics which are methods used to achieve an immediate or short-term goal. Strategy is essential since it forms the framework of all our actions serving as the guiding principle to our aspirations. It lays a clear path on how we plan to achieve our goals, thereby providing clear focus on what matters most. It provides a directional map that helps prevent us from veering off course and keeps us focused. This potent tool also aids in decision making, providing a clear perspective that allows us to make informed choices. Moreover, it can help in resource allocation, ensuring that efforts and resources are directed towards areas that will yield the most impact. Without a solid strategy, our actions become sporadic, diluting the power of our execution and jeopardizing the realization of our goals.

5.2. Setting the Groundwork for Strategy Formation

Before we delve into actual strategy formation, we need to have a succinct understanding of our objectives and the resources at our disposal. Thus, setting the groundwork means evaluating ourselves and our environment realistically. This involves:

1. Identifying Personal Goals - Start by clearly defining what it is you want to achieve. What are your long-term objectives and aspirations? Be specific.

2. Setting Sub-Goals - Break down your goals into smaller, attainable objectives.

3. Identifying Resources - What tools and resources do you have or need to accomplish these goals? This could include your skills, knowledge, experience, time, and physical resources.

4. Understanding the Situation - Take stock of your current circumstance, be it the financial situation, personal commitments, or time constraints.

5.3. The Art of Formulating Strategy: Crafting Your Blueprint for Success

Having laid the groundwork, we move to the intricate process of formulating a winning strategy. This commitment to strategic planning is integral for successfully navigating our path to breakthrough living.

1. Choose the Right Approach - Consider the options you have to reach your goal and select the one that is most aligned with your capabilities and resources.

2. Prioritize Actions - Not all actions carry the same weight,

prioritize ones that have the greater impact on your goal.

3. Develop an Implementation Plan - Formulate a detailed plan incorporating all your actions, assign schedules and deadlines.

4. Prepare for Challenges - Anticipate potential obstacles and plan solutions or alternatives for them in advance.

5.4. Making Your Strategic Plan Flexible and Adaptable

While maintaining a robust structure for our strategy is crucial, it's equally important that our strategic plan is flexible, adaptable, and agile. This ensures that in the face of changing circumstances, unanticipated challenges, or fresh opportunities, our strategic framework can swiftly pivot, re-align, and evolve without undermining the core objective.

5.5. Reviewing and Refining Your Strategy Regularly

Continual checks, reviews, and updates form a cardinal part of strategic planning. Monitor your progress, evaluate the effectiveness of your strategies, and be prepared to refine and adjust as needed. Could a strategy be improved? Was an obstacle overlooked? Answers to such questions will help you to build a stronger and more effective plan towards your objectives.

It is important to underscore that the strategy blueprint is not set in stone; it's an evolving design that moves and adapts according to the progression of our journey. No strategy is perfect right from its inception and requires modifications and refinements as per the course.

Strategy formation is thus a phase that demarcates the abstract from the concrete, the dream from the plan, and the destination from the journey. With a cogent strategy fueling your endeavor, you're all set to transition into a life defined by breakthroughs and substantial growth. Remember, it's not the most intelligent or the strongest who prevail, but those who navigate their course with an invincible strategy!

Chapter 6. Unleashing Potential: Growing Your Skills and Abilities

Your potential, limitless in nature, stands as the expansively vast, uncharted territory whose exploration will elucidate the course to your transformative success. This journey of unearthing and magnifying your capacities entails the thorough comprehension, acute identification, consistent nurturing, and meticulous honing of your skills and abilities. An alternate, potent perspective might instruct you to picture yourself as a fertile terrain awaiting the seeds of capability to be sown, nurtured, and evolved into a verdant panorama of expertise.

6.1. Deciphering Potential

Potential, as vast and elusive as it may seem, can be decrypted as the untapped potency to learn, develop and excel. It is that dynamic fusion of various abilities and capacities that are yet to be fully leveraged, constantly evolving in sync with the flow of knowledge, changes in perspective and novel challenges. Stating it succinctly, your potential is an amalgamation of all that you could possibly be and achieve, once you set into motion the wheels of sustained learning and concerted effort. It's getting familiar with the expanse of your chartless terrain, understanding its richness and depth, and discovering how far it can stretch when nurtured with the right care and effort.

6.2. Discovery: Uncovering Your Latent Skills and Abilities

There is a repository of dormant potential within you awaiting discovery. This potential is manifested in the form of skills, talents, and abilities, some conspicuous to your conscious mind, others obscured by the dust of unawareness. To transform these latent skills into prominent powerhouses, you must first embark on a journey of self-discovery. Get asking yourself what are the skills you possess that distinguish you within your sphere? Which abilities of yours have been commended in the past? Reflect closely on your life experiences and gather every traceable evidence of your distinguishing skills and abilities. You might surprise yourself at the plethora of talents you have hitherto remained unconvinced of, or oblivious to.

6.3. Fostering a Growth Mindset

To flourish your potential into tangible success, the soil of a fertile mindset is indispensable. The growth mindset refers to the cognitive frame where you perceive challenges as opportunities, where failures are not terminations, but points of learning, where your abilities are mouldable and upgradeable, and where every snag, hiccup, or bumble forms an integral part of your journey towards proficiency. It is the belief in your ability to enhance your abilities through perseverance and effort. Engagement, consistency, and optimistic resilience are the watering cans aiding this mindset evolve. Understand that your skills are not fixed. Like a seedling turning into a sturdy tree bearing fruit, your abilities too can expand, mature and ultimately multiply your level of success, given you nurture them with the right mindset.

6.4. The Art of Skill Amplification

Once the latent talents are discovered and the ground is prepared with a growth mindset, the next critical stage involves the deliberate imparting of deliberate and systematic learning. Comprehend the prerequisite knowledge, master the foundational skills, and gradually mount up to more complex abilities, thereby layering your expertise like an overfolding puff pastry. Explore and engage in diverse learning platforms like interactive content, practical projects, challenging assignments, constructive peer reviews, and immersive learning environments to amplify your skills. Also, remember, learning is not an isolated event but a social process. So, seek constructive feedback, encourage skill sharing, and promote collaborative learning.

6.5. Cultivating Resilience

The journey to potential maximization is not devoid of obstacles, setbacks, and failures. Resilience becomes your guiding star. It's the capacity to bounce back from adversities with more vigour and tenacity. It is about adapting well in the face of adversity, trauma, tragedy, threats, or significant sources of stress. To foster resilience, power through hardships with optimistic perseverance, create strong support systems, engage in regular self-care and mindfulness practices, and maintain a healthy work-life balance.

6.6. Continuous Improvement: Adopting the Kaizen Approach

The cyclical process of potential actualization doesn't rest at one-time achievement. The Kaizen approach, an embodiment of continuous improvement, involves making incremental advancements consistently to perpetually enhance output. To multiply success, always have a scope to get a step better at what you do, gradually but consistently growing in your skills and venturing beyond your comfort zone.

You are an endless reservoir of potential waiting to be tapped, stretched, and amplified. By adopting this comprehensive approach, fostering a growth mindset, and keeping an open mind for continuous learning and growth, one can take significant strides towards unleashing their true potential and multiplying success.

Chapter 7. Overcoming Failure: Reshaping Adversity into Advantage

Commencing an exploration of failure might, at first, feel akin to trudging through dense undergrowth, a murky thicket of disappointment, embarrassment, or even incidents of genuine heartache. However, the objective of this chapter is not to cower within the shadowy gloom of past defeats. Rather, we're embarking on a transformative journey, delicately unpicking the stitches of each setback to discover the strength, wisdom, and opportunities woven into the fabric of these experiences.

7.1. The Anatomy of Failure

Humanity's complex relationship with failure precedes recorded history, with every era marked by countless stories of ruin and redemption. However, in dissecting the anatomy of failure, we look less for historical context or psychological explanations, and more on a pragmatic framework which lays bare the raw components constituting this universally shared experience.

Failure typically occurs when our actions or decisions do not yield the desired outcome. It's that straightforward, albeit hard to accept. Anything we invest our effort, time, or resources into, from a basketball shot to a multinational corporation's launch, harbors the potential for failure if it doesn't deliver the anticipated results. Deriving from this fundamental understanding is a powerful revelation: Failure is not isolated to you, nor is it a permanent brand etched onto your identity. It's merely a detached event which indicates the need for tactical shifts or improvements.

7.2. Embracing Failure: The Launchpad for Growth

Embracing failure may seem counterproductive, akin to cherishing a thorn lodged in your side. But enchantingly, herein resides a fundamental transformation awaiting your grasp. Denying failure or succumbing to its emotional blow cultivates a cycle of stagnation and self-recrimination. Alternatively, acknowledging the occurrence and embracing its implications is analogous to the operation that removes the thorn, albeit painful but ultimately relieving.

When we transform our perspective to view failures as lessons or opportunities for growth rather than damning verdicts on our abilities, we catapult ourselves onto a trajectory of accelerated learning and adaptation. Every failed venture becomes a training module, a hands-on learning experience providing both theoretical knowledge and practical insights that textbooks cannot encapsulate. Had Thomas Edison dismissed his numerous unsuccessful attempts at inventing the light bulb as indicative of his incompetence, we might still be fumbling in the dark today.

7.3. The Power of Resilience

Akin to a knotted rope scaling a towering edifice, resilience is the lifeline formidable enough to pull us out from immersive pits of failure. Not only does it help counteract the immediate effects to our self-esteem, but it also equips us with an unyielding spirit to try again, rallying our resources for another round in the face of defeat.

Resilience shouldn't be mistaken for sheer stubbornness, though. It's a nuanced understanding of what went wrong, followed by a strategic modification in our next attempts. This potent combination of indefatigable determination and adaptability ultimately molds us into individuals who aren't dissuaded by the mere prospect of failure, resorting instead to take it in stride.

7.4. One Step Back For Two Steps Forward: The Framework

Our relationship with failure is not merely a psychological endeavor. It necessitates practical strategies to leverage these experiences. Here, we present a four-step framework for transforming adversity into an advantage.

1. Acknowledgement: Recognize the failure without blaming or criticizing yourself. It's an event that occurred, not a reflection of your worth or potential.

2. Analysis: Identify the precise reasons for failure. Was it a flaw in strategy, inadequate resources, or unforeseen circumstances? An honest audit helps you pinpoint the improvement areas.

3. Adaptation: Evolve your plan or approach based on your analysis. Redirect resources, hone skills, or modify strategies as necessary.

4. Action: Implement your new plan with enthusiasm and commitment. Stay open to feedback and adjust as you go along.

7.5. Where Failure Meets Success

At a confluence where the murky waters of failure blend with the roaring cascades of success, we find a potent elixir of Personal Evolution. The transformation of failure into success isn't a miraculous phenomenon, nor is it the plot of an inspiring movie. It's simply the trajectory that accepting, understanding, and leveraging failure rewards us.

The sculpting of success frequently demands the raw material of failure. It's a recasting process that fashions setbacks into springboards, and lapses into lessons. As we acquire the capability to reframe failure as a stepping stone towards success, we liberate ourselves from the fear of impending stagnation.

Failure might arrive cloaked in shades of defeat, but beneath the grayscale hues, it is the vibrant palette from which the Masterpiece of Success is sketched upon the canvas of our lives.

By resolutely reshaping adversity into advantage, you're inviting a profound transformation into the realm of infinite growth, and thereby embracing the promise of "Breakthrough Living".

Chapter 8. Consistency and Persistence: The Key to Long-Term Success

Beginning any journey entails encountering the thrilling buzz of novelty, igniting the simmering embers of enthusiasm, and harnessing the fiery passion that fizzles out self-doubt. The incandescent thrill of starting something new is electrifying, almost palpable. Yet, the true testament of any pursuit lies not in its initiation, but in its perpetuation — the commitment to consistency and the dedication to dogged persistence. In this chapter, we delve deeply into understanding these two pivotal aspects of long-term success: Consistency and Persistence.

8.1. The Power of Consistency

Consistency is known to many, but mastered by few. It is a discipline, an oft-underrated disposition that sets apart the successful from the ordinary. In understanding its power and potential, let us consider the metaphor of water dripping on a stone. A single droplet, in isolation, possesses a seemingly insignificant potency. Yet, it's the consistent, unrelenting cascade of these droplets over time that can carve the hardest of stones. Similar is the weight of our consistent actions. Individually, these actions may seem unnoticed and unimportant. Cumulatively, they build a reservoir of influence and accomplishments. Consistency, my dear reader, is the secret ingredient to the longevity of success. It molds habits, builds character, and above all, paves the path to your lasting success.

8.2. The Anatomy of Persistence

The second pillar of this triumphant twosome is Persistence.

Galvanizing enough, the word 'persistence' is more than a simple term. It is a relentless spirit, a resolute attitude that incites you to persist even when the going gets tough. Persistence is the causeway that transcends obstacles. It is the unwavering will that withstands the strong winds of failure and disappointment by holding the sails of hope steadfast. To persist is to not just withstand, but also to sustain and to prevail. Persistence, in all its forms, is a testament to human resilience and perseverance.

8.3. Achieving Consistent and Persistent Behavior

topic The Principle of Incremental Progress

You may wonder, "How can one harness the power of these two propellers of success?" One invaluable technique is by leveraging the principle of incremental progress, more commonly known as the 'Kaizen' principle. Kaizen, a Japanese philosophy, unearths the magical prowess of small, continuous improvements accumulated over time. This principle encourages you to move forward, however small the step might be, but to keep moving forward consistently, thereby employing the potency of both consistency and persistence.

topic The Implementation Intention Formula

The implementation intention formula is another instrumental tool that aids to embed consistency and persistence in your behavior. Pioneered by psychologist Peter Gollwitzer, this formula encapsulates the format of "In situation X, I will do behavior Y to achieve goal Z." This formula helps you specify your action, determine your context, and link them to your bigger goals, thereby reinforcing repeated behaviors in designated situations.

8.4. Allow Time to Play its Part

As you arm yourself with consistency and adorn the armor of persistence, remember to allow Time her dance. Remember that Rome wasn't built in a day, nor are empires of success. Just as a sculpture needs chiseling, a painting needs strokes, your life masterpiece needs time. Time renders maturity to your processes, refines your strategies, and magnifies your growth. Albeit slow, be patient as Time unfurls her magic. The growth you seek is oftentimes not linear but exponential. Allowing Time to play her part is honoring the processes that take you towards your goal.

8.5. Building Your Consistency and Persistence Muscle

topic Start Small, Win Big

Start small and aim for consistency in those small wins. Our brains are wired to respond to rewards. A pattern of small wins triggers a positive feedback loop in our brain, reinforcing the behavior and making it more likely for us to repeat those actions.

topic Cultivate Grit

Inculcate the intrinsic trait of grit, the insatiable appetite for long-term goals that combines passion and persistence. It's the tenacity to stick with your objectives, undeterred by hurdles and failures.

topic Maintain Consistent Self-Talk

Maintain a positive dialogue with yourself, a persistent whisper that says, "Keep going! You're on the right track."

topic Leverage the Power of Habit

Formulate habits that foster consistency and persistence. Remember, we are what we repeatedly do.

topic Embrace Failure as Your Tutor

Failures and setbacks will come your way. Instead of treating them as roadblocks, see them as tutors. Learn from each obstacle and persist in your journey.

Consistency, fused with the mettle of persistence, is a formidable force to reckon with, powering you towards your ultimate triumph. When embraced in their purest form and harnessed diligently, they hold the endurance to move mountains, to transform the seemingly impossible into the possible, and to unlock the unprecedented charm of long-term success. It is through the lens of consistency and persistence, you'll come to see the colors of your efforts, washed with the hues of trueness and importance, radiating into a spectrum of success that was once unfathomable, but now lies within your reach and reality.

So, dear reader, set your foot, affirm your grip, and propel yourself on the path of consistency and persistence. Therein lies the key to converting your wildest dreams into your tangible reality.

Chapter 9. Networking and Relationships: Building Your Success Ecosystem

The foundation of any successful journey is rooted not only in individual mastery and skill development but as well in the relationships you cultivate and the networking strategies you employ. In this chapter, you will explore the vast expansiveness of networking and the crucial role relationships play in your success ecosystem. Success is not a solitary process; it is one that necessitates the interweaving of diverse connections and relationships, which collectively contribute to an ecosystem that fosters and amplifies success.

9.1. The Power of Networking

A sizeable part of accelerating personal success stems from effective networking. Networking is not merely adding people to your contact list or attending social occasions. It's about building relationships and forming bonds with others. The relationships you nurture can lead to partnerships, mentorship, or sometimes just unique perspectives that help broaden your own understanding of success and its essence.

In a successful ecosystem, every organism has a role to play in the balance and growth of the system. Similarly, your relationships and networks form an essential part of your success ecosystem. Every contact, each relationship, contributes to your growth, provides different viewpoints, and introduces opportunities that you might not have been able to access alone.

The significance of networking lies in the strength of weak ties. Though it may seem counterintuitive, our most innovative and ground-breaking ideas often come from individuals from different walks of life—those weak ties that we may not frequently interact with but bring to the table distinct insights and expertise.

9.2. Building on Reciprocity

Relationships thrive on the principle of give and take. When networking, make it a priority to give before you ask. What you give doesn't have to be tangible; it might consist of your time, knowledge, or skills. It's about fostering a bond built on reciprocity, encouraging a fluid exchange of value.

Networking should ideally be a symbiotic process. Everyone has something unique to offer, be it advice, a skillset or a connection to another potential associate. When you approach networking from a standpoint of being of service, you not only build a healthy relationship but also cast yourself in a reliable and compassionate light. This builds your reputation as a key player in your network, further drawing opportunities your way.

9.3. Cultivating Relationships: Quality Over Quantity

In building your ecosystem, don't focus on quantity alone. A network built on numerous, shallow connections cannot compare to one fostered with fewer, yet deep and substantial relationships. Every interaction should be intentional, strengthening the bonds between you and your contact. The quality of your networks often determines the richness of opportunities available to you.

9.4. The Hidden Potential of Social Media

In the digital age, social media platforms have emerged as powerful networking agents. Leveraging platforms like LinkedIn, Twitter, and Facebook can help to identify and connect with people who share your goals or are on similar journeys. The potential embedded in these platforms is immense.

To unlock the hidden networking potential of social media, follow leaders and influencers in your field, join relevant groups and post meaningful content. Engage actively through comments, shares, and private messages. However, remember that the virtual world should complement and not replace real-life, face-to-face interactions. Employing a hybrid strategy can lead to a more diversified and resilient network.

In conclusion, networking is more than meets the eye and extends far beyond the initial greeting or exchange of business cards. It entails building and cultivating relationships over time, prioritizing quality over quantity, and the harmonious balance of giving before receiving. Remember, your network becomes your net worth. By creating a thriving and dynamic ecosystem of diverse relationships and connections, you set the stage for breakthrough living, enabling an environment that nurtures your goals and blooms with infinite potential.

Chapter 10. Multiplying Success: Strategies for Sustainable Growth

Strategic growth and success multiplication is not something that spontaneously happens. It necessitates thoughtful preparation, hard work, determination, modification, and continuous learning. It is a cyclically upward spiral of success. Just as a flower cannot bloom continuously without nurturing its roots, and an athlete cannot continue to succeed without continually honing their skills, it's the same with personal and professional success. In this chapter, we're going to delve into the art and science behind sustainable growth strategies that multiply your achievements.

10.1. The Nature of Sustainable Growth

Let's start by breaking down this key phrase into its components. Sustainability and growth, when combined, indicate a trajectory of progress that is not only rapid and substantial but also managed in a manner that ensures its longevity. Sustainable growth isn't about today's achievements but rather about the perpetual cycle of reaching new heights tomorrow, next week, next year, and many more years after that. You're not just in it for the quick wins — instead, you're building an enduring legacy of success.

Sustainable growth has certain hallmarks:

- It's planned: It's not accidental or lucky; it's carefully thought through and strategized.

- It's scalable: It doesn't crumble under increased demand or growth.

- It's resilient: It can weather storms and find the silver lining in clouds of failure.

- It's flexible: It adapts readily and elegantly to change.

10.2. From Success to Success

Once you have tasted success, it is important to sustain and build upon it. Consider your initial success as planting a successful seed. Now comes the truly challenging yet gratifying part: cultivating the offshoots, helping them grow into strong trees.

Every achievement (big or small) unlocks new possibilities and creates a positive cycle of success. Fueled by this success, you can continue to expand your comfort zone, unleash your hidden potential, and continue growing. It's about transferring the energy and momentum of an accomplishment to propel you towards conquering your next goal.

10.3. Achieving Growth through a Growth Mindset

Developing a growth mindset is the principal shift towards multiplying and sustaining success. Coined by psychologist Carol Dweck, a growth mindset is the belief that our talents and abilities can be developed through dedication, hard work, smart strategies, and input from others. It contrasts with a fixed mindset, which believes that talents and abilities are static traits, unchangeable, and unaffected by effort.

Cultivating a growth mindset helps you:

- Embrace challenges as growth opportunities.

- Persist in your efforts despite obstacles.

- View effort as an essential part of mastering a craft.

- Learn from criticism and feedback.

- Find inspiration in the success of others.

By encouraging a growth mentality, we remain open to continuous learning, flexibility, and progress, which inherently leads to sustainable success.

10.4. Designing a Sustainable Growth Strategy

Designing a sustainable growth strategy isn't a trivial task. It necessitates careful planning, continuous adjustment, and elevated perseverance. Begin by envisioning where you want to be in the foreseeable future. Set SMART goals (Specific, Measurable, Achievable, Relevant, and Time-Bound), evaluate your current position to identify gaps, and devise a roadmap to guide you from where you are to where you want to be.

Include constant learning and skill development in your roadmap. Life is, after all, a never-ending process of learning. We must continuously cultivate and refine our skills, abilities, knowledge, and attitudes, in line with our goals and aspirations.

Develop supportive habits and routines. Reinforce those habits until they become part of your day-to-day life, perpetuating success. From healthy eating, regular exercising, to lifelong learning – these habits impact your personal growth, well-being, and consequently, success.

10.5. Leverage Your Network for Growth

Having a robust network of professional and personal contacts is vital for sustainable growth. Connections provide you with diverse perspectives, widen your horizons, and offer opportunities for collaboration. They can mentor you, challenge you, and provide invaluable feedback, fostering your personal and professional growth. Moreover, surrounding yourself with a pool of positive, ambitious individuals can work wonders for your morale and motivation.

Remember, your network is your net worth. Invest time and energy in nurturing these relationships. Engage with your network regularly, offer assistance when possible, and keep the communication lines open.

10.6. Overcoming Barriers to Sustainable Growth

Obstacles and setbacks are inevitable on the path to sustainable success. Everyone encounters them, but it's your reaction that differentiates you from the rest. Instead of seeing these roadblocks as failure, view them as opportunities for learning and growth. Actively seek solutions, adjust your strategy, refine your skills, and continue moving forward with a positive, resilient outlook.

10.7. Embracing the Unknown: Constant Adaptability

Being adaptable involves staying open to new possibilities, ideas, and changes, and being willing to alter your approach when needed. It's about embracing the unknown rather than being fearful of it. Change, after all, is the only constant in life. By embracing change and persisting through failures, you foster a resilience that supports long-lasting success.

Sustainable growth is synonymous with long-term success.

Understand the nature of sustainable growth, develop a growth mindset, design your growth strategy, leverage your network, conquer barriers, and embrace adaptability to multiply your success manifold. This isn't the end of your journey, rather it's just the beginning. The true fruits of sustainable growth and success will become abundantly clear over time as you continue to thrive and grow.

Chapter 11. Embracing the Breakthrough Life: Your New Normal

Living a breakthrough life isn't about a one-time triumph or passing stream of advancements. In actuality, it's about making that lifestyle where every day is a possibility to reap the benefits of new accomplishments, to push past boundaries, and to live exceptionally. Succinctly put, embracing the breakthrough life is letting go of the old, ordinary, and low-impact existence to make space for a thriving, vibrant new normal. The ultimate test of all your efforts, in truth, lies in the ability to sustain what you have achieved and use it as a springboard to reach even higher heights.

11.1. Rooting Out Old Habits to Make Way for the New

Central to embracing the breakthrough life is establishing a deep-rooted habit of pushing beyond your comfort zone. Old habits die hard, they say—and indeed, that's precisely what makes the process so challenging. But the true essence of groundbreaking living is the capability to push those boundaries and, in doing so, keep raising your personal bar of achievement. In order to eliminate detrimental habits like procrastination, fear, or indecisiveness, an immense level of self-awareness is required.

Practicing mindfulness, keeping a journal of your behavioral patterns, or seeking help from a trusted mentor might just provide you with the insights needed to identify and address these damaging habits. Once identified, deploying counteractive measures. Whether it's commitment to your goals, resilience during setbacks, or resourcefulness in the face of adversity, these positive habits hold power to displace the old, obsolete ones which once held you back from your full potential.

11.2. Risk-taking: An Essential Ingredient of Breakthrough Living

Risk-taking is one of the quintessential attributes of a break-through life. The courage to take risks—calculated and otherwise—is precisely the disruptive factor required to overthrow stagnation and redundancy. To truly embrace a life abounding with recurring breakthroughs, one needs to eradicate the fear associated with the unknown.

Uncertainty is a part and parcel of life, and it's high time we made peace with it. Taking risks could sometimes result in setbacks or failure, but shying away from them only stagnates personal growth and success. Embrace the potential that you possess, see the risks for what they truly are: opportunities trickled with the promising potential of utmost success.

11.3. Lifelong Learning: Key to Sustained Success

A breakthrough life is a tapestry, intricately woven from the threads of knowledge, learning, and evolution. Remaining open to learning is the cornerstone of sustained personal development and success. The pace of today's ever-evolving world demands a mindset keen on learning and a willingness to adapt.

Whether it's enrolling for an online course to learn a new skill set, or reading a self-help book for enriching insights, every effort towards learning and self-improvement plays a crucial role in your growth. One must strive to keep pace with technological advancements, and continously be on the lookout to upgrade one's knowledge and skills through any medium available.

11.4. Embracing Wholeness: Balancing Success with Well-Being

While embracing a breakthrough life is primarily geared towards career and financial success, it doesn't mean forgoing the various other aspects of life—relationships, spiritual growth, mental and physical health—which are equally important. It's vital to understand that true success doesn't arise from imbalances; rather, it's born out of wholeness.

Taking time for self-reflection and fruitful rest, maintaining a healthy work-life balance, dedicating time to nourish personal relationships, and caring for your mental and physical health are all as essential as the pursuit of your goals.

11.5. Becoming a Beacon: Encouraging Others to Embrace Breakthrough Living

One of the most fulfilling aspects of achieving breakthrough living is the ability to inspire others to do the same. Having walked this path, navigated through its thorny undergrowth and emerged successful, you now possess the power to illuminate the path for others. Mentorship, guidance, or even simply leading by example can often prove instrumental in encouraging others to undertake this journey, thereby multiplying the impact of your breakthrough living.

To conclude, embracing a breakthrough life is more than simple high achievement—it's your ability to redefine 'success' itself. It's about decimating self-imposed limits and building a life that continually jolts you with invigorating challenges and immense opportunities for unprecedented success. It's about transforming your everyday living into an extraordinary existence and making that 'extraordinary' your new normal.